TENNESSEE

TENNESSEE

HELLO U.S.A.

by Karen Sirvaitis

Lerner Publications Company

You'll find this picture of a tulip poplar leaf at the beginning of each chapter in this book. The tulip poplar tree was adopted as the Tennessee state tree in 1947. Tulip poplars can grow to be 200 feet tall, and their trunks often stretch 50 to 100 feet without branches. Early pioneers in Tennessee used tulip poplars more than any other kind of wood to build houses, barns, and other buildings.

Cover (left): Stage set at the Grand Ole Opry in Nashville. Cover (right): A fire observation post in Great Smoky Mountains National Park. Pages 2–3: Pipe Organ rock formation in Cumberland Caverns. Page 3: Memphis skyline.

This book is available in two editions:
Library binding by Lerner Publications Company, a division of Lerner Publishing Group
Soft cover by First Avenue Editions, an imprint of Lerner Publishing Group
241 First Avenue North
Minneapolis, MN 55401 U.S.A.

Website address: www.lernerbooks.com

Library of Congress Cataloging-in-Publication Data

Sirvaitis, Karen, 1961–
    Tennessee / by Karen Sirvaitis (Rev. and expanded 2nd ed.)
        p.   cm. — (Hello U.S.A.)
    Includes bibliographical references and index.
    Summary: Presents the geography, history, people, places, and economy of Tennessee.
    ISBN: 0–8225–4090–8 (lib. bdg. : alk. paper)
    ISBN: 0–8225–0795–1 (pbk. : alk. paper)
    1. Tennessee—Juvenile literature. [1. Tennessee.] I. Title. II. Series.
F436.3 .S58 2003
976.8—dc21   2001008653

Manufactured in the United States of America
1 2 3 4 5 6 – JR – 08 07 06 05 04 03

CONTENTS

Rich, fertile farmland covers much of Middle Tennessee.

THE LAND

Three States in One

Walk through Tennessee from west to east and you'll cross gently rolling hills, fertile farmland, and miles of misty mountains before completing your journey. The state has three land regions, commonly called West, Middle, and East Tennessee. Because these regions look so different, Tennessee has been described as three states in one.

Tennessee is located in the southeastern United States. Shaped almost like a rectangle, the state has two natural boundaries—the Mississippi River in the west and the Appalachian Mountains in the east. Eight states border Tennessee. They are Kentucky, Virginia, North Carolina, Georgia, Alabama, Mississippi, Arkansas, and Missouri.

Raccoons are common in Tennessee.

Clarksville

Tiptonville

Nashville

Murfreesboro

Spring Hill

Jackson

Shelbyville

Manchester

Memphis

Pulaski

South Pittsburg

Dayton

Chattanooga

Norris

Knoxville

Gatlinburg

Pigeon Forge

Kingsport

Jonesborough

Great Smoky
Mountains
National Park

TENNESSEE
Political Map

⭐ State capital

0   25   50 Miles

0   25   50   75   100 Kilometers

The drawing of Tennessee on this page is called a political map. It shows features created by people, including cities and parks. The map on the facing page is called a physical map. It shows physical features of Tennessee, such as mountains, rivers, and lakes. The colors represent a range of elevations, or heights above sea level (see legend box). This map also shows the geographical regions of Tennessee.

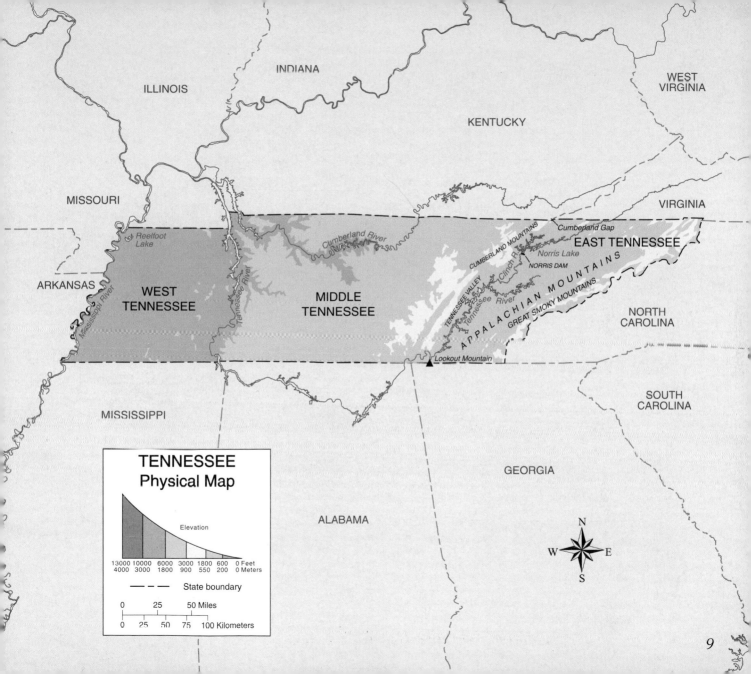

ILLINOIS

INDIANA

WEST VIRGINIA

MISSOURI

KENTUCKY

VIRGINIA

ARKANSAS

Reelfoot Lake

Cumberland River

Cumberland Gap

CUMBERLAND MOUNTAINS

EAST TENNESSEE

Norris Lake

NORRIS DAM

WEST TENNESSEE

Mississippi River

Tennessee River

MIDDLE TENNESSEE

TENNESSEE VALLEY

Clinch R.

Tennessee River

A P P A L A C H I A N   M O U N T A I N S

GREAT SMOKY MOUNTAINS

NORTH CAROLINA

Lookout Mountain

MISSISSIPPI

SOUTH CAROLINA

GEORGIA

ALABAMA

TENNESSEE
Physical Map

Elevation

13000	10000	6000	3000	1800	600	0 Feet
4000	3000	1800	900	550	200	0 Meters

- - - State boundary

0   25   50 Miles

0   25   50   75   100 Kilometers

N
W E
S

Tennessee's westernmost region, called West Tennessee, is a plain with rolling hills, wide valleys, and flatlands. Two major rivers, the Mississippi and the Tennessee, fence off the plain from bordering states and from Middle Tennessee.

The Tennessee River runs through both West and East Tennessee.

Middle Tennessee holds a large **basin** (a wide, bowl-shaped dip in the earth's surface). Many farmhouses and crops are found in this fertile area. **Plantations** (large farms) were once common in the basin, which has been called the Garden of Tennessee. The land along the eastern edge of the basin gradually slopes upward to meet the foothills of the Appalachian highlands.

Middle Tennessee's basin area contains excellent soil for farming.

The Great Smoky Mountains rise high over East Tennessee. The Smokies create a natural border between Tennessee and North Carolina.

The foothills mark the beginning of East Tennessee. A wide valley separates the foothills from the Appalachian Mountains, the oldest mountain chain in North America. These mountains rose from the earth's crust millions of years ago. Some of the major Appalachian mountain ranges in Tennessee include the Great Smoky Mountains (Smokies) and the Cumberland Mountains.

Three major rivers flow through Tennessee. The Mississippi, in West Tennessee, is the longest river in the United States. The Cumberland River cuts a jagged path through the northern half of Middle Tennessee. The Tennessee River, which begins in the Appalachians, loops down through Alabama before reentering Tennessee in the west.

A riverboat steams its way down the Mississippi River. The Mississippi forms the border between Tennessee and neighboring states Missouri and Arkansas.

There are many lakes in Tennessee. Reelfoot, one of the state's natural lakes, was born in 1811 when an earthquake sank a large piece of forest in northwestern Tennessee. The violent trembling also forced the Mississippi River to flow backward for a short period of time. The river quickly flooded the sunken woodland. When the ground stopped shaking, the river returned to its course, leaving behind a large lake.

Cypress trees soak in Reelfoot Lake. The trees are the only remains of an old forest.

Norris Dam on the Clinch River, which flows into the Tennessee River, is one of the dams built by the Tennessee Valley Authority (TVA). Its reservoir, Norris Lake, is one of the Great Lakes of the South.

More lakes were created starting in 1933. A U.S. government organization called the Tennessee Valley Authority (TVA) began building a series of dams and locks on some of Tennessee's rivers. Each of these dams holds back water, creating a **reservoir,** or artificial lake. The dozens of reservoirs in Tennessee are known as the Great Lakes of the South.

The dams did more than create recreational lakes. They also raised the water level in shallow places, so that large ships and barges can navigate the rivers. The dams provide a cheap source of electricity for the Tennessee Valley area, and they control flooding caused by heavy rains.

Huge TVA dams stop flooding and hold water for irrigation.

The TVA's Stairway

Picture the Tennessee River flowing down a huge stairway, each dam acting as a step. Some of the dams created by the TVA (Tennessee Valley Authority) have a lock. A lock permits ships, barges, and recreational boats to cross the dam. When a boat moving downstream reaches a dam, it enters the lock, a water-filled chamber with gates at both ends. While the gates are closed, the boat waits until the water level is lowered to match the water level downstream, just beyond the lock. The boat can then continue its journey. The TVA operates a system of 39 dams and locks throughout the valley. Some of the dams run by the TVA are located in states next to Tennessee.

Heavy rains do occasionally pound Tennessee, but the state's climate is generally not harsh. Middle Tennessee gets the most rain. Throughout much of the state, snowfall is light and the snow usually melts quickly. East Tennessee receives more snow than other parts of the state.

During the summer, temperatures average more than 80° F in West Tennessee, which is the hottest region. The mountainous areas of East Tennessee are somewhat cooler. During the winter, temperatures throughout the state seldom drop below freezing.

In the spring, flowering shrubs of azalea and laurel brighten mountain slopes. Hickory, pine, oak, and poplar trees forest about half the state. The U.S. national bird, the bald eagle, nests in the forests of East Tennessee and in the marshes of Reelfoot Lake.

In the winter, great blue herons join the eagles, flocking to cypress trees that sprawl in the lake. White-tailed deer, black bears, foxes, beavers, and raccoons also make their homes in Tennessee.

A white-tailed deer listens closely for possible danger.

Native Americans lived off the land in the Tennessee area by hunting and gathering and, later, by farming.

THE HISTORY

A Military Tradition

Little is known about the first peoples to live in the area that later became Tennessee. By about 14,000 years ago, Native Americans were living in the area. These people hunted, fished, and gathered berries and hickory nuts for food.

Eventually, the Indians began to grow their food. They planted gardens of beans, squash, and corn. By A.D. 1000, they settled in the area and used grasses and brush to build homes in villages. These Indians are known as Mound Builders. Some of the Mound Builders were expert farmers. Others were master craftspeople.

Mound Builders
created earthen
temples for worship.

The Mound Builders are best remembered for their earthen temples and burial mounds. By hauling load after load of dirt on their backs, the Mound Builders eventually moved tons of soil and stones to temple sites. Some of the structures they built are still standing.

No one knows exactly what happened to these Indians, but by the mid-1500s mound building had stopped. Different Indian cultures came to the area. The Cherokee settled in Middle Tennessee. The Chickasaw entered West Tennessee.

The Cherokee built villages of as many as 50 log houses along rivers in the foothills of the Great Smoky Mountains. The Cherokee were skilled hunters and farmers. Corn was their most important crop.

The Chickasaw lived near the Mississippi River, which often flooded, so they built their villages on high ground. Crops grew well in the area's rich, black soil, and the surrounding forests made excellent hunting grounds. Expert fishers, the Chickasaw often enjoyed meals of catfish.

In 1540 the Indians of Tennessee welcomed into their villages a Spaniard named Hernando de Soto. De Soto, the first European to explore what later became the southeastern United States, was searching for gold. For months he and his army lived among the Native Americans, who fed the newcomers and invited them to tribal celebrations.

Hernando de Soto first landed in Florida. He explored the area that later became Alabama, Mississippi, Arkansas, Oklahoma, and Louisiana, where he died.

The Spaniards did not return the Indians' kindness. When de Soto was ready to leave the area, he planned to take some Indians as slaves. Indian warriors tried to stop de Soto. These Indians attacked the Spaniards, killing many of them.

But the Indians suffered more. De Soto and his army had brought an enemy the Indians could not overcome—disease. By the time the Spaniards left in 1541, hundreds of Indians had died from smallpox and other illnesses.

Europeans did not return to the Tennessee area until the late 1600s. Starting in the 1670s, explorers from several European countries came to the area. To reach what would become Tennessee, some of these adventurers paddled down the Mississippi River in canoes. Others walked across the Appalachian Mountains. After these explorations, three European countries—France, Great Britain, and Spain—claimed the Tennessee region.

Cherokee and Chickasaw lands and areas farther east had been claimed by Britain. The British government set up several **colonies** along the

Atlantic coast in these territories. The colony of North Carolina reached inland to include all of what later became Tennessee.

By the late 1700s, colonists from North Carolina and Virginia had begun trekking over the Appalachian Mountains into Tennessee. They settled in the wilderness, far from any cities, and had little or no contact with the people they left behind. The pioneers were independent. They made log cabins, horseshoes, spinning wheels, quilts, tables, chairs—almost everything they needed

Cumberland Gap, a mountain pass in northeastern Tennessee, provided a passageway for pioneers traveling westward. In the 1770s, Daniel Boone *(leading horse)* led hundreds of travelers through the passageway.

Handmade crafts, such as quilting, remain an Appalachian tradition.

To the pioneers who ventured west of the Appalachians, the Atlantic coast seemed far away. But the future of the pioneers was tied to events that were happening in the East. The British government was charging the colonists taxes on everyday items such as tea and sugar. The colonists believed that since they were not represented in the British government, the taxes were unfair. In 1775 the angry colonists began fighting the British in a war called the American Revolution. Pioneers in the Tennessee area were eager to go east to fight the British. But the war soon came to them. Tennesseans also fought the Cherokee, who had sided with the British. The British had promised to help the Cherokee stop pioneers from moving onto the Indians' land.

In 1783 Britain lost the war. The 13 freed colonies formed their own nation—the United States of America.

After the revolution, the Union created territories out of land west of the Appalachians. A territory had less power than a state, but once it had enough people, a territory could become a state. In 1789 the Tennessee region became the Territory of the United States South of the River Ohio.

Some early settlers in Tennessee established small farms that had several outbuildings for livestock and crop storage.

Davy Crockett

Ten years before Tennessee gained statehood, a boy named Davy Crockett was born in Greene County. At that time, Tennessee was the American frontier—land to which few white people had ventured.

Davy Crockett was well suited to the times. During his boyhood, he learned how to fire a hunting rifle with amazing accuracy. As a young man, Crockett won hundreds of shooting contests.

Crockett used his skill with firearms to hunt bears and raccoons. He made clothing, rugs, and blankets out of the skins. He fed his family and his neighbors with the meat.

Davy Crockett

Davy Crockett loved to hunt, but he also loved to tell stories. Many of them were tall tales (exaggerations). For instance, Crockett once claimed to have killed 105 bears in one season! His friends, however, believed that Crockett was a much better storyteller than he was a hunter.

Crockett's ability to conquer the frontier and still have a sense of humor helped to make him famous. Davy Crockett died in 1836. Since then, generations of Americans have heard his stories and have tried to understand what it would be like to be a pioneer in Tennessee.

The territory's population soon grew to more than 60,000 white people—more than enough to apply for statehood. A large chunk of the territory adopted a constitution and took the name of a Cherokee village called *Tanasie*, or Tennessee. In 1796 Tennessee became the 16th state to join the Union. It was also the first state to be created from a U.S. government territory.

While Tennesseans were settling into statehood, the United States entered into another war with Britain. The War of 1812 was fought over trading rights. The U.S. government asked citizens to volunteer as soldiers. Thousands of Tennesseans signed up to fight. This enthusiasm earned Tennessee the nickname the Volunteer State.

One volunteer was Andrew Jackson. General Jackson led a successful attack against the British during the Battle of New Orleans. Jackson became a hero. His popularity swept across his home state of Tennessee, and he decided to run for president. He was elected in 1828 and became the country's first president from the West.

Andrew Jackson became the seventh president of the United States. Tennesseans boasted that Jackson was the first U.S. president born in a log cabin.

Jackson served in the White House for eight years. During his presidency, settlers demanded more Indian land. Jackson believed that Americans and Native Americans could not live together peacefully. In 1830 he approved the Indian Removal Act. This law stated that Indians living east of the Mississippi River would have to move to Oklahoma, a territory west of the river.

The Indian Removal Act broke many **treaties** the U.S. government had made with Native Americans. In 1838 the Chickasaw and most of the Cherokee were forced to walk to Oklahoma. So many Indians died from hunger and disease that the journey is called the Trail of Tears.

The Trail of Tears

In 1838 the U.S. government forced thousands of Indians to move to reservations in Oklahoma. Their journey became known as the Trail of Tears. Many of these Indians were Cherokee, Chickasaw, Choctaw, Creek, or Seminole—known by white settlers in the 1800s as the Five Civilized Tribes. Many people of the Five Civilized Tribes tried to adopt the lifestyle of the white settlers. But despite the Indians' efforts to fit in and to keep peace, white people still wanted their land. On the Trail of Tears, the people of the Five Civilized Tribes realized they had given up their traditions only to have to give up their homes and, in many cases, their lives.

Slave traders advertised
their services to attract buyers.

After the state's Indians were gone, Tennesseans had the land they wanted. But another conflict was brewing. During the 1800s, many slaves had been brought to Tennessee from Africa. The Northern states had already outlawed slavery. In most of the South, however, plantation owners still used slaves to work the land. The owners said slavery was necessary to make a profit.

Other Southern states depended on slaves more than Tennessee did. When the U.S. government threatened to end slavery across the nation, some of these states decided to leave the Union. They formed a new country—the Confederate States of America. In the Confederacy, slavery was legal.

Many Tennesseans were against slavery. They voted to stay in the Union. But when Abraham Lincoln, then president of the United States, sent troops to the South in 1861, Tennesseans immediately offered to help the Southern cause. Volunteers from the state lined up to fight against the North.

Volunteer troops from Tennessee supported the Confederacy. These Confederate soldiers are playing dominoes to pass the time.

In 1862 in West Tennessee, Union and Confederate soldiers fought the Battle of Shiloh. About 24,000 soldiers were killed or injured during the battle. Named after a church on the battlefield, the battle marked a Union army victory and helped the North gain control of the Mississippi River as far south as Memphis, Tennessee.

The Civil War began in April 1861. Tennessee was hit hard and fast by Union troops. Forts Henry and Donelson near Nashville were taken in 1862, while they were still under construction. Later that same year, Union forces took the city of Memphis in the Battle of Shiloh, one of the bloodiest of the war.

The Union controlled Tennessee but not without a struggle. Confederate soldiers often attacked Union holdings, attempting to regain control. The fighting was fierce and frequent. Of all the states, only Virginia saw more battles than Tennessee did.

In 1865 the Civil War ended in victory for the Union. The slaves had been freed, but they, along with other Southerners, still faced many hardships. Tennessee's crops and orchards had been burned. Its farms and mansions were destroyed. Many Tennesseans had lost their lives.

Many buildings, farms, and forts were destroyed during the Civil War. This fort near Knoxville, Tennessee, was leveled by Union attacks.

During the Reconstruction period after the Civil War, lumber was taken from East Tennessee to help rebuild the South.

During a period called **Reconstruction,** the U.S. government began to rebuild the South. Northerners also made laws to readmit Confederate states to the Union. On July 24, 1866, Tennessee, the last state to leave the Union, became the first state allowed to rejoin.

While Tennessee's farmers were starting to grow crops again, more and more factories were being built. By the early 1900s, many Tennesseans were moving off their farms and into the state's cities, such as Nashville, Knoxville, and Memphis, to find work in manufacturing.

The Monkey Trial

Tennessee gained worldwide attention during the Scopes trial of 1925. John Thomas Scopes was a teacher in Dayton, Tennessee. Scopes taught his high school class that human beings developed from primates, which include monkeys and apes.

Not everybody agreed with this scientific point of view, known as the theory of evolution. At the time, discussing evolution in a public school was illegal in Tennessee because the belief went against the teachings in the Bible. John Scopes was arrested.

Scopes's case was tried in court and became known around the world as "The Monkey Trial." The judge said Scopes was guilty and had to pay a $100 fine to the state. Later, however, the decision was reversed. Tennessee changed the law in 1967, making it legal to teach evolution in the classroom.

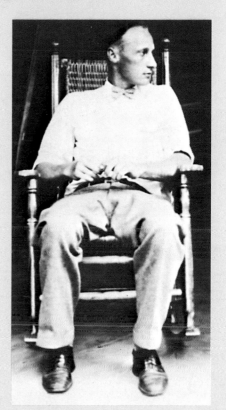

John Scopes

By the 1930s, jobs had become hard to find because of the Great Depression, a major slump in the country's economy. But in 1933, the Tennessee Valley Authority (TVA) began building dams, creating jobs for hundreds of Tennesseans. Although the TVA employed many of the jobless, it also upset many people.

For the dams to be built, some Tennesseans had to move off land their families had lived on for years.

The TVA's dams helped to control flooding in Tennessee.

In 1940 Chickamauga Dam was completed in Hamilton County, Tennessee. The dam's lock allows ships and freighters to navigate the river.

Farmhouses were torn down. Water from the dams' reservoirs permanently flooded these properties. Despite many arguments against the dams, the projects were completed. The modern-day TVA operates 39 dams within the Tennessee Valley.

The Ku Klux Klan (KKK) started in Pulaski, Tennessee. The KKK is sometimes violent toward black people and other groups whose beliefs differ from those of the Klan.

In the 1950s and 1960s, the state faced new challenges. African Americans in Tennessee and many other states had long faced discrimination and unfair treatment. Black people wanted the same **civil rights** (personal freedoms) white people had. Working together in the civil rights movement, many Americans protested laws that treated blacks unfairly.

Some protests in Tennessee were peaceful. Others became violent. Martin Luther King Jr. was a civil rights leader who wanted people to protest peacefully. While visiting Memphis in 1968, King was shot and killed. His death sparked several riots. In that same year, the government passed a new civil rights law that treated blacks and other minorities more fairly.

Since then Tennesseans have strived to make their state a place where all people are welcome to live and work. By the 1980s and 1990s, Tennesseans were working to build the state's struggling economy. In 1982 Knoxville hosted a world's fair to promote tourism and attract new industry. In 1985 the Tennessee-Tombigbee Waterway project connected the Tennessee River to the Gulf of Mexico. The new passage helped stimulate economic growth.

Former vice president Al Gore was born in Carthage, Tennessee.

As the state works to build its future, it also remembers its past. In 1996 Tennessee celebrated the bicentennial of its statehood, honoring the people who helped create the Volunteer State.

In 2000 Vice President Al Gore, a native Tennessean and former senator, ran for president against George W. Bush. Although Bush defeated Gore, the race was one of the closest in U.S. history. Many Tennesseans continue to take pride in Gore's political accomplishments.

Memphis's Beale Street, a hot spot for musical performers, brings together members of Tennessee's diverse ethnic groups.

PEOPLE & ECONOMY

A Proud Heritage

Tennesseans are proud of their rich history. The state's 5.6 million people come from several different ethnic backgrounds. About 81 percent of Tennesseans have European ancestors. Many are descendants of the first English settlers to come to the area. Other **immigrants** (newcomers) came from Germany, Ireland, and Scotland.

African Americans make up about 16 percent of Tennessee's population. About 2 percent of the population is Latino. Other minority groups are much smaller, making up 2 percent of the population. Only about 15,000 Tennesseans are Native American.

A small number of Tennesseans make a living just as their ancestors did—by farming the land. About 4 percent of all jobs are in agriculture, but this small number grows a lot of food. Farmland covers nearly half of Tennessee. Livestock farmers raise cattle, hogs, and sheep throughout Middle Tennessee, where much of the land is good for grazing.

Cotton, Tennessee's most valuable harvest, grows best in the climate and soil of West Tennessee. Soybeans and tobacco, the state's other major crops, grow in East and Middle Tennessee. Tomatoes, snap beans, cabbages, apples, peaches, and strawberries are also raised throughout the state.

Manufacturing employs about 16 percent of Tennessee's workforce. Many factory employees make chemical products, such as paints, medicines, and soaps. Other people work with food products in meat-packing plants or canning factories.

Farmers in East and Middle Tennessee grow tobacco.

TENNESSEE
Economic Map

The symbols on this map show where different economic activities take place in Tennessee. The legend below explains what each symbol stands for.

	Beef cattle		Copper		Forest products		Hogs		Popcorn		Soybeans		Tourism
	Berries		Corn		Fruit		Manufacturing		Potatoes		Stone		Vegetables
	Clay		Cotton		Grapes		Marble		Poultry		Sweet potatoes		Wheat
	Coal		Dairy products		Hay		Peanuts		Sheep		Tobacco		

Many of Tennessee's factories, like this one in Kingsport, make chemicals and plastics.

While the state leads the country in the production of zinc, mining employs less than 1 percent of Tennessee's workers. Miners dig for several minerals, including coal and phosphate rock.

Sixty-two percent of Tennessee's workers hold service jobs. Services include jobs as tour guides, bankers, salesclerks, and doctors. Most people who have service jobs live and work in Tennessee's cities. The largest cities in the state are Memphis, Nashville, Knoxville, and Chattanooga.

Memphis, in West Tennessee, is the state's largest city. The city's hospitals, along with its many health-care professionals and research scientists, help make health care the leading industry in Memphis.

The Memphis skyline towers above the Wolf River. Memphis is Tennessee's largest city.

Beale Street, in Memphis, is known as the home of blues music. Memphis was also the home of Elvis Presley, a singer who since the 1950s has been called the King of Rock and Roll. Presley died in 1977, but his mansion, Graceland, is visited by more than 600,000 fans every year.

Music is also big business in Middle Tennessee. Nashville, the state's capital, is the home of country

Thousands of fans visit singer Elvis Presley's grave *(right)* at Graceland every year. The gates to Graceland *(below)* are decorated with musical notes.

Visitors to Opryland, U.S.A. take a ride on the Old Mill Scream.

music. A section of the city is called Music Row. Dozens of music publishing companies and recording studios line the district's 14 blocks. The Grand Ole Opry House, a theater and the world's largest broadcasting studio, lies just outside of Nashville in the popular theme park known as Opryland, U.S.A.

Tennessee walking horses often compete in horse shows.

Middle Tennessee is also famous for the Tennessee walking horse. This saddle horse is bred near Nashville. Because of their graceful step, Tennessee walking horses are comfortable to ride and are popular at horse shows.

The people of Tennessee are proud of their history. The Museum of Appalachia in Norris displays animal traps, butter churns, wagons, gourds (used as ladles), and hundreds of other items made by Tennessee's pioneers. Each October the museum sponsors the Tennessee Fall Homecoming. At this event, visitors can experience pioneer life by boiling molasses, driving oxen, or sewing quilts.

A worker at the Museum of Appalachia demonstrates how pioneers plowed their fields—with a mule and a hand plow.

Great Smoky Mountains National Park stretches across the border from Tennessee into North Carolina. Those who trek through this park can easily imagine what the first pioneers faced. Visitors camp in the woods, surrounded by ancient hardwood and red spruce forests. Each year, between 9 and 10 million people visit this wilderness, making it one of the most visited national parks in the United States.

Each year the Great Smoky Mountains attract millions of tourists to Tennessee.

Just outside Great Smoky Mountains National Park lies Gatlinburg. Nestled up against the Appalachian Mountains, Gatlinburg gets enough snow to attract skiers and is one of the southern-most ski resorts in the country. This quaint Appalachian town also features hundreds of shops that sell quilts, tinware, and other crafts—items once made by Tennessee's pioneers.

The Ober Gatlinburg Aerial Tramway, America's largest tram, carries passengers to Gatlinburg's ski resorts and indoor amusement park.

Tennesee's farms depend on the nutrients found in the state's topsoil, which can be washed away by wind and rain.

THE ENVIRONMENT

Stopping Soil Erosion

The Appalachian Mountains in Tennessee once looked quite different. They were taller and had sharper peaks. But over millions of years, wind and rain have been working away at the mountains, wearing them down to their present height.

Rain and wind cause erosion of land all over the world. People in Tennessee are particularly concerned about the **erosion** of the **topsoil** on the state's farms. Soil erosion can be a threat to the food supply. When soil erosion occurs naturally, it is usually a very gradual process. As rain falls, some of it collects on the ground and flows across the earth's surface. The flowing rainwater, called runoff, carries loose soil into rivers and lakes.

Many Tennessee farmers raise strawberries.

Heavy rainfall pounding on unprotected soil, such as farmland, can create deep gullies.

Over years, runoff can carry tons of soil to a body of water. Soil erosion becomes a problem when people accelerate, or speed up, this naturally slow process.

Most accelerated soil erosion in Tennessee occurs on farmland, which covers about half the state. To prepare their lands for crops, farmers clear the trees and cut the grasses. The soil is then ready for planting, but it is also unprotected from rain and wind.

Because Tennessee has so much cropland, a lot of

soil is eroding quickly. If this rate of erosion keeps up, the rich topsoil on which Tennesseans depend to grow food will disappear into rivers and lakes.

In the Tennessee Valley, almost 60 percent of the soil is highly erodible. To help save soil from erosion and to protect precious farmland, the U.S. government passed a law called the 1985 Farm Bill. To meet the goals of this law, farmers in Tennessee and other states have worked to reduce the amount of soil lost to erosion each year.

Flowing rainwater carries soil into rivers, making them muddy.

To be healthy, crops need the nutrients found in topsoil.

Farmers use several methods to slow the negative effects of erosion. **Crop rotation,** or changing the types of crops planted every few years, helps keep the soil rich in nutrients. When the same crops are planted year after year, they rob the soil of nutrients.

Another way to reduce soil erosion is to plant trees on farmland whose soil has become too poor to grow crops. The leaves of a tree act as an umbrella, protecting soil from harsh rains. A tree's roots help to hold soil in place. Trees and other plants also absorb rainwater, reducing runoff.

Many of Tennessee's farmers have started to practice what is called **conservation tillage.** After a crop has been harvested, farmers leave the dying plants to cover the soil, protecting it from wind and rain. When they are ready to plant again, farmers use a machine to drill holes for the seeds. The ground is not plowed or tilled. So the old, decaying crop continues to protect and add nutrients to the soil.

This farmer is planting corn in a field that has been protected using the conservation tillage method.

Tennesseans want to reduce soil erosion in their state, but the task is not easy. Farmers do not always practice some of the conservation methods because they are too costly. These methods include contour plowing and terracing, two special ways to structure a field to reduce runoff. And farmers who do practice conservation techniques sometimes end up getting fewer crops.

Contour plowing involves plowing across, instead of up and down, the slope of a hill to reduce soil erosion.

To make sure enough food reaches grocery stores in the future, farmers are changing the way they plant and harvest crops.

To help farmers conserve the land, researchers are developing new conservation techniques that cost less and that will produce as much harvest as the old methods. In addition, the government passed the 1996 Farm Bill to introduce new conservation measures and to step up current efforts. Tennessee has at least one resource that is needed to reduce soil erosion—people. Hundreds of Tennesseans have volunteered to help save their state's soil. Once again, Tennessee is living up to its nickname—the Volunteer State.

Fun Facts

The Seeing Eye, which opened in Nashville in 1929, was the first organization in the United States to train guide dogs for blind people. Buddy, a German shepherd, was the first Seeing Eye dog in America. She lived in Nashville with her owner, Morris Frank.

In 1886 Tennessee became the first state to have two brothers run against each other in an election for governor. Robert Love Taylor received more votes than his brother Alfred Alexander Taylor did, but Alfred was not to be left out. In 1920 he ran for governor again (not against his brother) and won.

Nashville resident Morris Frank was the first American to have a Seeing Eye dog. Here, Frank stands with his dog, Buddy.

Clarence Saunders of Memphis created the world's first supermarket. Saunders got the name for his market after watching a pig wiggle under a fence. He designed one long, winding aisle for the store and called it Piggly Wiggly.

Each year about 600,000 people travel to Memphis to visit Graceland, the former home of the King of Rock and Roll, Elvis Presley. After the White House, the mansion is the second most visited home in the United States.

After almost 75 years of broadcasts from Opryland, the Grand Ole Opry is the world's longest-running live radio program.

A temporary state called Franklin existed from 1784 to 1788 in what became eastern Tennessee. Although Franklin, named after Benjamin Franklin, had its own constitution and governor, the state was not formally recognized by the United States. The area became part of Tennessee in 1796.

STATE SONG

Tennesseans show their love of music in the fact that they have not one but six official state songs. In 1935 "When It's Iris Time in Tennessee" became the second song to be adopted by the state.

WHEN IT'S IRIS TIME IN TENNESSEE

by Willa Waid Newman

A TENNESSEE RECIPE

Each May, cities in West and Middle Tennessee host strawberry festivals. Strawberry bread is one of the many delicious ways Tennesseans enjoy the tasty fruit. Ask an adult to help with all steps involving an oven.

STRAWBERRY BREAD

You will need:

3 cups all-purpose flour
1 teaspoon baking soda
1 teaspoon cinnamon
2 cups sugar

1 teaspoon salt
4 eggs, well beaten
Two 10-ounce packages frozen strawberries
1¼ cups cooking oil

1. Mix flour, baking soda, cinnamon, sugar, and salt together.
2. Drain thawed strawberries. Stir eggs, strawberries, and oil together. Add to dry ingredients.
3. Mix until just moistened. Place dough in two greased and floured 9- by 5-inch loaf pans.
4. Bake at 350° F for 1 hour. Let cool for 10 minutes.

Makes two loaves.

HISTORICAL TIMELINE

12,000 B.C. Native Americans move into the region that later became Tennessee.

A.D. 1000 Mound Builders settle in the Tennessee area and construct temples.

1540 Spanish explorer Hernando de Soto arrives in what later became Tennessee.

1769 Famous frontiersman Daniel Boone travels through the Cumberland Gap.

1775 The American Revolution (1775–1783) begins; pioneers in the Tennessee area volunteer to fight for the colonies.

1796 Tennessee becomes the 16th state to join the Union.

1812 Volunteers from Tennessee fight in the War of 1812 (1812–1814).

1828 Tennessean Andrew Jackson is elected president.

1830 President Jackson approves the Indian Removal Act, forcing Native Americans onto reservations.

1838 Cherokee and Chickasaw Indians are forced to march from Tennessee to Oklahoma in what is later called the Trail of Tears.

1861 Tennessee joins the Confederacy in the Civil War (1861–1865).

1862 Union troops capture Forts Henry and Donelson near Nashville; Memphis falls to the Union during the Battle of Shiloh.

1866 Tennessee is the first Confederate state readmitted to the Union.

1925 High school teacher John Scopes is arrested for teaching evolution. His trial becomes known worldwide as "The Monkey Trial."

1933 Tennessee Valley Authority begins building dams along Tennessee's rivers.

1968 Civil rights leader Martin Luther King Jr. is assassinated in Memphis.

1982 Knoxville hosts the World's Fair.

1985 The Tennessee-Tombigbee Waterway links the Tennessee River to the Gulf of Mexico.

1996 Tennessee celebrates 200 years of statehood.

Julian Bond

Davy Crockett

Aretha Franklin

OUTSTANDING TENNESSEANS

Julian Bond (born 1940) is a civil rights leader and politician from Nashville. In 1968, while serving as a congressperson, Bond became the first African American to be nominated for the office of vice president of the United States. In 1998 Bond was elected chairperson of the National Association for the Advancement of Colored People (NAACP).

Davy Crockett (1786–1836), a pioneer who was born in Greene County, Tennessee, became a legend of the American frontier. The frontiersman, militiaman, and politician lived an extraordinary life before being killed at the Alamo during the fight for Texas's independence.

Dragging Canoe (1738?–1792) was a Native American leader who led a band of Cherokee Indians called the Chickamauga. Dragging Canoe refused to sign treaties with white people and fought pioneers who were moving into the Tennessee Valley.

Aretha Franklin (born 1942), known as the Queen of Soul, is a singer originally from Memphis. As a child, Franklin began singing in the church her father pastored. Franklin has won 15 Grammy Awards, and her hit records have sold millions of copies.

Albert Gore Jr. (born 1948), a politician from Carthage, Tennessee, served the state as a U.S. senator and congressperson. Gore was elected vice president of the United States in 1992 and 1996, and he was the Democratic nominee for president in 2000. Gore won the popular vote but lost the controversial election to George W. Bush.

Albert Gore Jr.

Alex Haley (1921–1992) was a writer who grew up in Henning, Tennessee, listening to tales of his African ancestry. He used the clues in these stories to find his African roots in a village in West Africa. After 12 years of research, Haley wrote the best-selling book *Roots*, which was made into a popular television miniseries.

Alex Haley

W. C. Handy (1873–1958) was a musician who introduced a new form of music called the blues on Beale Street in Memphis in the early 1900s. Known as the Father of Blues, he wrote hits such as "Memphis Blues" and "St. Louis Blues." Handy moved to Memphis in 1909.

W. C. Handy

Sam Houston (1793–1863) was a pioneer who settled in the mountains of Tennessee when he was 13 years old. At times he lived with Cherokee Indians. He later became a congressperson and then governor of Tennessee. Houston used his political position and his understanding of Indian affairs to help Native Americans.

Sam Houston

Andrew Jackson (1767–1845) became the seventh president of the United States. Jackson visited Middle Tennessee as a young man and decided to stay. He helped Tennessee become a state. Some believe he suggested that Tennessee be its name. Jackson, nicknamed "Old Hickory," was president from 1829 to 1837.

Andrew Johnson (1808–1875) was a politician who moved to Tennessee when he was a young man. As a congressperson, Johnson remained in the Senate even after Tennessee seceded. Because of his loyalty, President Abraham Lincoln made him governor of Tennessee. He was elected vice president of the United States in 1864. Johnson became president after President Abraham Lincoln was assassinated in 1864. He served as president from 1865 to 1869.

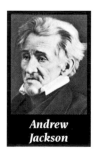

Andrew Jackson

Dolly Parton

Minnie Pearl

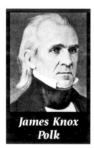

James Knox Polk

Elvis Presley

Carey Estes Kefauver (1903–1963) was a U.S. senator who became a candidate for vice president in the 1956 presidential election. Kefauver, from Madisonville, Tennessee, is often remembered for the coonskin cap he sometimes wore.

Dolly Parton (born 1946) sings and writes country and pop-rock music. She grew up in Locust Ridge, Tennessee, and went on to Nashville to become a star. Parton has also acted in several movies, including *Nine to Five* and *Steel Magnolias.*

Minnie Pearl (1912–1996), a comedienne, was named Sarah Colley at birth. Pearl, who was a regular on shows such as the *Grand Ole Opry* and *Hee Haw*, always appeared wearing a straw hat with its price tag dangling from the brim. She was born in Centreville.

James Knox Polk (1795–1849) was a politician who settled with his family in Maury County, Tennessee, when he was 11 years old. After serving as governor of Tennessee, Polk was elected president of the United States in 1844. During Polk's presidency, much of the West became part of the United States.

Elvis Aaron Presley (1935–1977) was a legendary rock-and-roll singer. Born in Mississippi, Presley moved with his family to Memphis at the age of 13. Known as the "King of Rock and Roll," Elvis had many hit songs, including "Hound Dog" and "Love Me Tender." During his career, Presley sold millions of records and acted in many movies.

John Crowe Ransom (1888–1974) was a poet and critic born in Pulaski, Tennessee. He believed that people could be happy only by leading a simple life. His volumes of poems include *Poems about God, Chills and Fever,* and *Grace after Meat.*

Oscar Robertson (born 1938), a basketball player, was born in Charlotte, Tennessee. During his 14 years as a professional basketball player with the Cincinnati Royals and the Milwaukee Bucks, Robertson averaged more than 25 points per game. He also helped the 1960 U.S. Olympic team win a gold medal.

Wilma Rudolph (1940–1994) was an athlete from Clarksville, Tennessee. Rudolph overcame the crippling effects of polio to become a runner and eventually went on to win gold medals at the 1956 and 1960 Olympic Games. After retiring from track, she started the Wilma Rudolph Foundation to help underprivileged athletes.

Wilma Rudolph

Sequoyah (1776?–1843) was a Cherokee Indian born near Tuskegee, Tennessee. He invented the first alphabet for an Indian language. Among his people, Sequoyah was honored for his leadership. The California redwood tree carries his name.

Sequoyah

Cybill Shepherd (born 1950) is an actress from Memphis. Some of her most famous roles include the 1971 film *The Last Picture Show* and its 1990 sequel, *Texasville.* From 1985 to 1989, Shepherd also costarred in the popular television series *Moonlighting.* She starred in her own television show, *Cybill,* from 1995 to 1998.

Cybill Shepherd

Lynn Swann (born 1952), a former football player, brought excitement to many Super Bowl games while playing with the Pittsburgh Steelers. Swann, who was born in Alcoa, Tennessee, set many records and was named to the Pro Football Hall of Fame. After retiring from football in 1982, he became an announcer for ABC Sports.

Lynn Swann

FACTS-AT-A-GLANCE

Nickname: Volunteer State

Songs: "My Homeland, Tennessee," "The Pride of Tennessee," "Rocky Top," "Tennessee," "Tennessee Waltz," and "When It's Iris Time in Tennessee"

Motto: Agriculture and Commerce

Flower: iris

Tree: tulip poplar

Bird: mockingbird

Wild animal: raccoon

Horse: Tennessee Walking Horse

Gem: Tennessee River pearl

Insects: firefly and ladybug

Date and ranking of statehood: June 1, 1796, the 16th state

Capital: Nashville

Area: 41,219 square miles

Rank in area, nationwide: 34th

Average January temperature: 38° F

Average July temperature: 78° F

Tennessee's state flag was adopted in 1905. The three stars in the center represent West, Middle, and East Tennessee.

POPULATION GROWTH

Millions

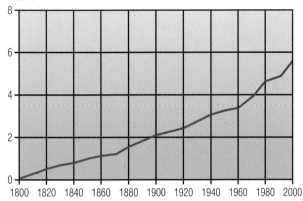

This chart shows how Tennessee's population has grown from 1800 to 2000.

Population: 5,689,283 (2000 census)

Rank in population, nationwide: 16th

Major cities and populations: (2000 census) Memphis (650,100), Nashville (545,524), Knoxville (173,890), Chattanooga (155,554), Clarksville (103,455), Murfreesboro (68,816), Jackson (59,643)

U.S. senators: 2

U.S. representatives: 9

Electoral votes: 11

Natural resources: coal, limestone, marble, natural gas, petroleum, phosphate rock, soil, stone, water, zinc

Agricultural products: apples, beef cattle, cabbages, cotton, dairy cattle, hogs, peaches, sheep, snap beans, soybeans, strawberries, tobacco, tomatoes

Manufactured goods: chemical products, clothing, electronic equipment, food products, machinery, plastic products, transportation equipment

Tennessee's state seal was officially adopted in 1987. The plow, wheat, and cotton stand for agriculture, and the riverboat represents trade. The date 1796 is the year Tennessee received statehood.

WHERE TENNESSEANS WORK

Services—62 percent (services includes jobs in trade; community, social, and personal services; finance, insurance, and real estate; transportation, communication, and utilities)

Manufacturing—16 percent

Government—12 percent

Construction—6 percent

Agriculture—4 percent

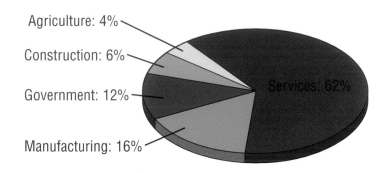

Agriculture: 4%
Construction: 6%
Government: 12%
Manufacturing: 16%
Services: 62%

GROSS STATE PRODUCT

Services—61 percent

Manufacturing—22 percent

Government—12 percent

Construction—4 percent

Agriculture—1 percent

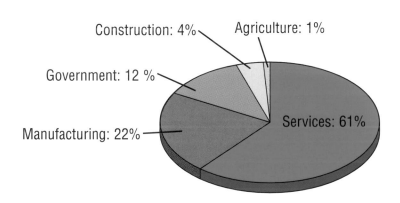

Construction: 4%
Agriculture: 1%
Government: 12 %
Manufacturing: 22%
Services: 61%

TENNESSEE WILDLIFE

Mammals: beaver, black bear, fox, gray bat, mountain lion, raccoon, squirrel, white-tailed deer

Birds: bald eagle, blue heron, mockingbird, peregrine falcon, raven, wild turkey, woodthrush

Amphibians and reptiles: American toad, box turtle, cave salamander, green frog, timber rattlesnake, western cottonmouth

Fish: bass, crappie, lake sturgeon, trout, walleyed pike

Trees: ash, cherry, cypress, elm, hickory, pine, poplar, maple, red oak, white oak

Wild plants: azalea, dragonroot, iris, mountain laurel, passionflower, rhododendron

Peregrine falcon

PLACES TO VISIT

Country Music Hall of Fame, Nashville
Live entertainment, interactive exhibits, and a museum are a few of the highlights visitors can enjoy.

Cumberland Science Museum, Nashville
Interactive exhibits and events help visitors explore the world of science. The museum includes Sudekum Planetarium.

Dollywood, Pigeon Forge
This theme park, named for singer Dolly Parton, features Smoky Mountain crafts, country music concerts, and rides.

Graceland Mansion, Memphis
Visitors to Elvis Presley's 14-acre estate can learn more about the life and career of the "King of Rock and Roll."

Great Smoky Mountains National Park, East Tennessee
One of the largest protected areas in the eastern United States, the park offers tourists a chance to see various plants and animals, mountain views, and ancient artifacts.

Lookout Mountain, near Chattanooga
Visitors to the historic site can ride the Incline Railway up the mountain to see one of the most famous Civil War sites. Rock City Gardens and Ruby Falls offer scenic views.

Mud Island River Park, Memphis

A museum, amphitheater, and gardens are some of the reasons visitors are attracted to this park located on the Mississippi River. A scaled-down model of the river from its headwaters to its mouth is also on display.

Museum of Appalachia, Norris

The museum features Native American artifacts and exhibits about life in the Southern Appalachia region.

Music Valley Wax Museum, Nashville

Located across from the Opryland Hotel, the museum houses the wax figures of more than 50 country music stars.

Old Stone Fort State Archaeological Area, Manchester

This 2,000-year-old Native American site features mounds and areas that served as ceremonial gathering places for more than 500 years.

Parthenon, Nashville

Built for Tennessee's 1897 centennial exposition, this is the only full-scale replica of the Parthenon, an ancient landmark in Athens, Greece. The building also houses artwork by American painters and temporary exhibits.

Tennessee Aquarium, Chattanooga

The world's largest freshwater aquarium is home to more than 9,000 aquatic creatures from the world's river systems.

The Parthenon, in Nashville

ANNUAL EVENTS

Reelfoot Eagle Watch Tours, Tiptonville—*January–March*

Smoky Mountains Storytelling Festival, Pigeon Forge—*February*

Dogwood Arts Festival, Knoxville—*April*

National Cornbread Festival, South Pittsburg—*April*

Tennessee Strawberry Festival, Dayton—*May*

Riverbend Festival, Chattanooga—*June*

Country Music Fan Fair, Nashville—*June*

Tennessee Walking Horse National Celebration, Shelbyville—
August

Tennessee State Fair, Nashville—*September*

Smoky Mountain Harvest Festival, East Tennessee—
September–October

National Storytelling Festival, Jonesborough—*October*

Christmas at Graceland, Memphis—*November–January*

LEARN MORE ABOUT TENNESSEE

BOOKS

General

Barrett, Tracy. *Tennessee.* New York: Benchmark Books, 1997.

Weatherly, Myra S. *Tennessee.* Danbury, CT: Children's Press, 2001.

Special Interest

Alphin, Elaine Marie. *Davy Crockett.* Minneapolis: Lerner Publications Company, 2003. A biography of Tennessee's legendary pioneer.

Arnold, James R., and Roberta Wiener. *River to Victory: The Civil War in the West 1861–1863.* Minneapolis: Lerner Publications Company, 2002. Covers the Civil War, including the participation of Tennesseans.

Behrman, Carol H. *Andrew Jackson.* Minneapolis: Lerner Publications, 2003. Learn more about the Tennessee pioneer who became one of the nation's most powerful leaders.

Hanson, Freya Ottem. *The Scopes Monkey Trial: A Headline Court Case.* Hillside, NJ: Enslow Publishers, 2000. Read about the trial that changed American education. For older readers.

Sherrow, Victoria. *Wilma Rudolph.* Minneapolis: Carolrhoda Books, 2000. A biography of the woman who overcame the crippling effects of polio to win three gold medals in the 1960 Olympics.

Fiction

Bradley, Kimberly Brubaker. *Weaver's Daughter.* New York: Delacorte Press, 2000. Ten-year-old Lizzy Baker has moved to the Tennessee area in the 1790s. Lizzy must make a hard choice: stay with her family in Tennessee or move to North Carolina to help her asthma.

Brummett, Nancy Parker. *The Journey of Elisa: From Switzerland to America.* Elgin, IL: David C. Cook Publishing Co., 2000. Eleven-year-old Elisa and her family face hardship and hope when they move to Tennessee to be near relatives.

Crist-Evans, Craig. *Moon Over Tennessee: A Boy's Civil War Journal.* Boston: Houghton Mifflin, 1999. This fictional journal tells the story of a 13-year-old Tennessee boy who accompanies his father to fight in the Civil War.

Crofford, Emily. *When the River Ran Backward.* Carolrhoda Books, 2000. A young girl and her family struggle to survive the 1811 earthquake, tremors from which formed Reelfoot Lake in Tennessee.

Felder, Deborah G. *Changing Times: The Story of a Tennessee Walking Horse and the Girl Who Proves That Grown-Ups Don't Always Know Best.* New York: Scholastic, Inc., 1998. Lucy's is determined to keep her faithful horse, Clipper, despite her father's protest.

WEBSITES

Tennessee Anytime
<http://www.tennesseeanytime.org>
The Volunteer State's official website includes links to history, government, and business pages.

State of Tennessee Department of Tourist Development
<http://www.tourism.state.tn.us/>
Find festivals, events, and other Tennessee attractions.

Tennessean.com
<http://www.tennessean.com/
Read local, national, and world events from Nashville's online newspaper.

Tennessee Aquarium
<http://www.tennis.org/>
Take a virtual tour of the world's largest freshwater aquarium.

PRONUNCIATION GUIDE

Appalachian (ap-uh-LAY-chuhn)

Chattanooga (chat-uh-NOO-guh)

Cherokee (CHER-uh-kee)

Chickamauga (chick-uh-MAW-guh)

Chickasaw (CHIHK-saw)

de Soto, Hernando (dih SOH-toh, ehr-NAHN-doh)

Knoxville (NAHKS-vihl)

Mississippi (mihs-uh-SIHP-ee)

Seminole (SEHM-uh-nohl)

Shiloh (SHY-loh)

Nashville is home to Tennessee's state capitol building.

GLOSSARY

basin: a bowl-shaped region; all the land drained by a river and its branches

civil rights: the right of all citizens —regardless of race, religion, or sex—to enjoy life, liberty, property, and equal protection under the law

colony: a territory ruled by a country some distance away

conservation tillage: any method of plowing and tending fields that reduces the loss of soil and water on farmland

crop rotation: alternating the types of crops grown in a field from one year to the next so that minerals taken from the soil by one type of crop can be replaced

erosion: the wearing away of the earth's surface by the forces of water, wind, or ice

immigrant: a person who moves into a foreign country and settles there

plantation: a large estate, usually in a warm climate, on which crops are grown by workers who live on the estate. In the past, plantation owners often used slave labor.

Reconstruction: the period from 1865 to 1877 during which the U.S. government brought the Southern states back into the Union after the Civil War. Before rejoining the Union, a Southern state had to pass a law allowing black men to vote. Places destroyed in the war were rebuilt and industries were developed.

reservoir: an artificial lake where water is collected and stored for later use

topsoil: the surface layer of dirt in which plants grow

treaty: an agreement between two or more groups, usually having to do with peace or trade

INDEX

PHOTO ACKNOWLEDGMENTS

Cover: © Chase Swift/CORBIS (left), © James L. Amos/CORBIS (right); © Raymond Gehman/CORBIS, pp. 2–3 (both); © Kitty Kohout/Root Resources, pp. 4, 7 (inset), 19 (inset), 41 (inset), 53 (inset); © Buddy Mays/Travel Stock, pp. 6, 11, 13, 16; Lynn Troy Maniscalco, pp. 7, 24; Ron Bell, Presentationmaps.com, pp. 8, 9, 43; © David Muench/CORBIS, p. 10; Tennessee Tourist Development, pp. 12, 14, 17, 53 (right); © Mary A. Root/Root Resources, p. 15; Tennessee State Museum from a painting by Carlyle Urello, pp. 18, 20; Library of Congress, pp. 21, 31, 32, 33, 35, 36, 38, 67 (second from bottom and bottom), 68 (second from bottom); Washington University Gallery of Art, p. 23; Cumberland Gap National Historic Park, p. 25; Stock Montage/Superstock, p. 26; The Hermitage: Home of Andrew Jackson, Nashville, TN, p. 28; Woolaroc Museum, Bartlesville, Oklahoma, p. 29; Tennessee State Museum, pp. 30, 67 (second from top); Great Smoky Mountains National Park, pp. 34, 50; Chattanooga-Hamilton County Bicentennial Library, p. 37; © Robert Maass/CORBIS, p. 39; © Franz-Marc Frei/CORBIS, p. 40; Jeff Greenberg, p. 42; Eastman Chemical Company, p. 44; © Dennis MacDonald/Root Resources, pp. 45, 46 (right); © Elvis Presley Enterprises, p. 46 (left); Donnie Beauchamp, Opryland, U.S.A., p. 47; Voice of the Tennessee Walking Horse, p. 48; Robin Hood, Museum of Appalachia, Norris, Tennessee, p. 49; © Jan Butchofsky-Houser/CORBIS, p. 51; U.S. Army Corps of Engineers, Memphis District, p. 52; USDA, pp. 54, 56, 58, 59; Tim McCabe/USDA-SCS, p. 55; © Debra Ferguson/Ag-Stock USA, p. 57; The Seeing Eye, Inc., p. 60; Jack Lindstrom, p. 61; Orrin N. Alt Photography, p. 66 (top); Archives Division—Texas State Library. p. 66 (second from top); Atlantic Records Company, p. 66 (second from bottom); Clinton/Gore National Campaign Headquarters, p. 66 (bottom); Alex Gotfryd, p. 67 (top); David Gahr, p. 68 (top); Jim Halsey Co. Inc., p. 68 (second from top); Independent Picture Service, p. 68 (bottom); AP/Wide World Photos, p. 69 (top); Atlanta Historical Society, p. 69 (second from top); Hollywood Book and Poster Company, p. 69 (second from bottom); Pittsburgh Steelers, p. 69 (bottom); Jean Matheny, p. 70 (top); Laura Westlund, p. 70 (bottom); © Anthony Mercieca/Root Resources, p. 73; Nashville Area Chamber of Commerce, p. 75; © Phillip Wright/Visuals Unlimited, p. 80